Excel 2023

From Beginner to Expert | The Illustrative Guide to Master All The Essential Functions and Formulas in Just 7 Days With Step-by-Step Tutorials, Practical Examples, Tips & Tricks

By

Richard Wilson

Table of Contents

Introduction

Microsoft Excel is capable of saving and analyzing numerical and statistical data. It is a spreadsheet tool that you can use to do so. Computer calculations, graphing tools, pivot tables, macro programming, and other functions are all available in Microsoft Excel for a variety of purposes. It is compatible with a variety of operating systems, including MacOS X, Windows, Android, and iOS. An Excel spreadsheet is a table made up of columns and rows of information. In most cases, columns are allocated alphabetical letters, and rows are assigned numerical identifiers. A cell is defined as the point where two columns or rows meet. In a cell's address, the letter that represents a column and the number that indicates a row are combined to form a single number.

Those who deal with accounts and certain aspects of financial professions that require forecasting features with a combination of built-in capabilities can use this package as a very clever tool for their personal domestic/enterprise-level work performance, and they are fully qualified to use Excel in this capacity. As you may be aware, Excel is a component of Microsoft Office that is devoted to the computation, analysis, charting, and other spreadsheet solutions that are common in the business world. Informally known as ESS, it has been used in the past with programs such as LOTUS-123, VP Planner, VisiCalc, SUPER CALC, Quattro Pro, and a variety of other spreadsheet solutions. Although the premise of a spreadsheet is the same across all programs, the appearance and performance of each package varies greatly, with Excel being the most sophisticated spreadsheet solution currently available. Excel 2021 is a spreadsheet application that enables you to deal with data in a quick and accurate manner. Many of the functions are the same as those found in previous versions of Excel. In addition to different tools for organizing and updating data, it also provides charts for displaying data and other useful features. Consider the following scenario: you want to brush up on your Excel abilities, or you've never used it before.

In such a circumstance, this book will teach you how to use spreadsheet software to deal with rows, columns, data formatting, basic formulas, and functions, among other things. Excel 2021 introduces a few new features that you should take note of. There are a variety of topics covered, including text, arithmetic, and logical functions, among others.

Chapter 1: What Is Excel?

MS Excel is a spreadsheet application for Windows, macOS, Android, and iOS created by Microsoft. It includes calculating or computation skills, graphing tools, tables, and the Visual Basic for Apps macro programming language.

1.1 What Is Microsoft Excel?

Microsoft Excel is the most extensively used spreadsheet application on the market. Despite the fact Microsoft Excel's extensive features and powers might seem intimidating, the interface is straightforward and simple to use. Excel, on the other hand, can be learned in a short period of time, and after you've mastered the basics, mastering the more sophisticated aspects of the program is rather straightforward. When it comes to Excel, it is more than a spreadsheet program; it is also an app development environment that provides data analysis and presentation capabilities that go beyond those of a traditional spreadsheet. This means that thanks to the advantages of Excel, you may create a full, customized application that does precisely what you need it to do.

- Referencing other dialogue boxes shrinks the dialogue box to a more manageable size.
- Range dialogue boxes that allow range references may be entered more quickly.
- The wheel button on the new IntelliMouse gamepad is used to

scroll and zoom in and out.

- To relocate a range of cells to another workbook or worksheet window for easier drag-and-drop editing, drag the border of the range of cells to the desired location.

- As in earlier versions, you can save a list of workbooks.

- You may undo as many acts as you like up to the last 16 actions.

- In the case of exiting the document with several open files, the Save All option allows you to select whether or not to save all of the files before quitting.

- Closing a large number of files.

- The row or column titles will vary as you drag the spotlight for the current cell around the screen.

- The Full-Screen function is used to display a larger number of worksheets.

A list of active workbooks, their widths, and their placement are saved to a workspace file so that the screen looks just as it did the first time you accessed it from the File menu. All of the solutions listed above are completely compatible with all users and all of the other programs that are accessible to do the same work. Some Excel features, on the other hand, have been designed in such a manner that users may easily access them.

Below the image are some of its characteristics:

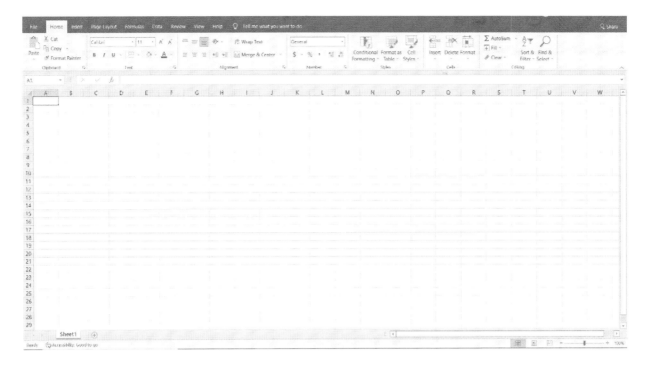

Calculation and examination:

The calculating and analytical functions of this program are so useful in practice that anybody can complete a project with ease, regardless of whether they are working with universal constant data or variable data. If, for example, several sheets are used to store all of the data associated with each cell or sheet, changing the data inside one cell or sheet would update the whole formulation, presenting the full dependent outcome.

Charting:

Using Excel's charting tool, you may quickly and easily generate charts with the most suitable features and with the lowest risk. It is possible to build charts in Excel that are completely integrated or nonembedded, which makes it possible to complete the process of modifying layouts, alignments, and other sorts of flexibility automatically.

Auto formatting with built-in functions:

The formatting of data may also be automated via the use of built-in functions. In this situation, users do not need to be concerned with the one-line process or any other aspects. In fact, the whole section is intended to be of assistance to the user.

Advanced query features:

As you may be aware, the cell is the most fundamental component of any worksheet. It contains all the data in the form of rows and columns or sheets, and query tools enable you to browse for records fast depending on the conditions you provide.

The following is the fastest and most straightforward interface between Office components and web-based data:

Because the integrated HTML editor handles the entire work for all users, the most recent feature of Excel enables you to complete the operation and connect the documents with one another based on any subject via intranet and the internet. You may add any text as a sub-information to any website without having to go via a third party.

Data processing on a large scale:

Let's see an example; consider that your firm has four branches, which in order to collect the production schedule report, you must link your database, which consists of worksheets and workbooks, and you must collect the actual production status from each of those branches. Excel's extensive capabilities make it possible to execute such work in a short period of time and efficiently.

Other Excel Features: Excel contains a number of additional features that help improve its overall functionality.

Specification: The following tasks are made easier with the use of Microsoft Excel 2022.

- Interpretation
- Providing financial solutions for forecasting
- Plotting
- Lookup tables that are complicated
- Data manipulation on the internet
- Data on the World Wide Web
- The exchange of information with other office households as well as with other applications.

Apart from that, while dealing with Excel to do practical activities, a user may experiment with a range of options. Let's start with the fundamentals of Excel before going on to more sophisticated subjects and functions.

1.2 History of Ms. Excel

Microsoft Excel has been in use since 1982 when it was initially presented as Multiplan, a world-famous CP/M (Control Software for Microcomputers) that was eventually supplanted by Lotus 1-2-3 on MS-DOS-based systems. As early as 1987, Microsoft released Excel v2.0 for Windows, and by 1988, the program had begun to outsell both Lotus 1-2-3 and the newly released QuatroPro. In 1993, Microsoft introduced Excel v5.0 for Windows, which contained VBA (Visual Basic for Applications) often known as Macros, which allowed users to create macros. This opened the door to almost limitless possibilities in the automation of repetitive operations like number crunching, process automation, and data presentation for commercial purposes. Moving forward to the present day, with the newest update of Excel 2019 and Excel365, Microsoft Excel is by far the most familiar and widely used early application in the world due to its ability to adapt to almost any business process. When combined with the usage of other Microsoft Office apps, such as Word, Outlook, PowerPoint, and so on, there is little that this very powerful combo cannot do. The possibilities for using Microsoft Excel as well as the Office Suite are virtually unlimited.

Take, for example, the following top ten list of the most popular and effective built-in Excel features:

- Almost any data may be modeled and analyzed with ease.
- Identify the most relevant data elements as rapidly as possible.
- In a single cell, you may create data plots.
- You may access your spreadsheet from almost any location.
- When people collaborate, they are able to connect, share, and achieve more.
- Take advantage of Pivot Charts, which are more interactive and dynamic.
- Bring a higher level of complexity to your data displays.
- Make things simpler and more efficient.
- Increase your computing power so you can create larger, more sophisticated spreadsheets.
- Excel Services allows you to publish and distribute documents.

When you combine this with the ability to personalize and automate any activity via the usage of Visual Basic for Applications (VBA), you have a wonderful value-added BI (Business Intelligence) system that is versatile and creative enough to address almost any business requirement. Are you interested in using Microsoft Excel to help with your business solutions? You can rely on Excel Help professionals. We've worked with companies of all sizes and across a wide range of industries. From famous brands to small businesses, we can assist you in streamlining your operations using Microsoft Excel as well as other Microsoft products and solutions.

Chapter 2: Getting Started with Excel

For novice Excel users, it is highly advised that they begin their learning process by following a systematic approach. If you're concerned about becoming a proficient Excel user, be sure you follow the steps outlined below to get there. Following the completion of these exercises, you should have a much greater understanding of the conceptual features of Microsoft Excel. The procedure is as follows:

- **Start the Excel Worksheet Session**

After starting an Excel session, it presents a set of spreadsheets with several rows/columns, and cells, all of which have been previously addressed, and it is prepared to deal with any data manipulation concerns that may arise. At this stage, you may begin inputting information. Including different fonts, colors, and scaling sizes, as well as linking data to the appropriate formula, among other things. A few activities will be handled automatically, but most of them will need to be completed manually in accordance with your criteria.

- **Using any number of sheets**

All of the information indicated above will be put into cells on a worksheet, which is only a portion of the space available. Excel offers you the choice of working with a single or several sheets of data. The user can organize the data in any way they see fit; if a financial or annual presentation includes summary data on the homepage, it is possible to have relevant metadata on a different place of the same worksheet or on a new worksheet. This is especially useful if the user wishes to complete all of the required tasks on the very same worksheet or on numerous sheets. By organizing data in any way the user sees fit upon request, the primary data will be computed and connected to the presentation's main page, where you'll have the option of finishing the assignment using simple data linking and hyperlinking to go within the text. In order to keep all of the information organized and segregated into sections that may be connected together, many sheets might be used.

- **Calculation**

Calculations will be carried out after the final compilation of the whole statement based on the data segments with the use of Formulae and Functions. Many functions and equations are pre-installed on the computer.

- **Save the file**

It is important that you save the data for future reference because it is necessary to preserve the current working state once the data has been entered and the calculations have been performed. It provides a few alternatives.

- **Worksheet Formatting and Formatting**

Users must be able to modify and format spreadsheets in order to alter and correct flaws in the information. For example, spelling fixes, data entering, and other similar tasks fall under the category of "editing". Formal formatting refers to the process of altering the appearance of any information in a spreadsheet.

- **Plotting**

In order to make the data presentation more understandable, the input data will be converted into a graph manner before being shown. If you are acquainted with the many types of graphs, it will be much simpler for you to finish this assignment with a reasonable notion.

- **Advanced problem solving**

Pivot tables as well as other unique capabilities are included in the advanced features, which may be used to show whole professional reports in a single presentation.

- **Interaction of Data with Other Members of the Office Family**

Using additional programs on the same system or on other platforms, you may make changes to the data you've input in different formats. In Word and PowerPoint, for example, Excel data may be transformed, linked, and hyperlinked with other documents and spreadsheets.

- **Excel web-based applications**

Using web-based apps, the web player or new web spectator may make use of the substantial potential of web-based applications, such as data entry on the web offline or online. The process could be completed fast if you take a brief look at the options accessible in Excel's menus before beginning. When we go into more detail, we'll go through some of the menu choices that are similar to those in Word, and also discuss the differences.

2.1 Where Do You Find Excel?

You can find Excel in the following places:

I. Using Microsoft Office on your home computer.

1) Excel may be found in the C: Program Files Microsoft Office folder. To open it, choose the "EXCEL" symbol from the toolbar. Alternatively, you may search for "EXCEL" using the search function available from the start screen on your desktop computer.

2) Once Excel is launched, you may need to import Solver into the spreadsheet. In the Excel main menu, choose "Tools" from the drop-down list. If you can locate Solvers in the Toolbar, you are ready to begin working with it. If you are unable to locate Solver in the Tools menu, move to Step 3 in this section.

3) The first step is to open Microsoft Excel and go to Tools>Macro>Security and set the Security level to medium; otherwise, you will not be able to go to Solver.

4) Next, go to C: Program Files Microsoft Office Library Solver and double-click "SOLVER," which will cause it to be immediately added to the Excel workbook. Alternatively, you may search for "Solver" using the search function available from the start screen on your desktop pc. When you click on "Solver," it will be instantly imported into Excel.

5) Return to Excel and check that Solver has been successfully installed. The solver may be found in the Toolbar by selecting the Excel Tools icon and then clicking on Solver.

II. On the MSCC's personal computers

1)   Navigate to C: Program Files Microsoft Office and double-click the program file "EXCEL" to open it.

2)   In the Excel taskbar, select Tools->Add-Ins from the drop-down menu.

3)   Set the "Solver Add-In" option in the Add-Ins dialogue box and then click "OK". The Solver tool will then appear in the Tools drop-down menu.

2.2 Excel File Extensions

Excel is one of the tools that allows us to save files in a number of different file types and extensions. The.xlsx extension is a frequently used extension in Excel, and is used for storing a basic form of data. In addition to XLS, there is another default extension that was used until Microsoft Office 2007. XLSM is a database that may be used to store VBA code. This is only intended for use with macros. An additional file extension, CSV Comma Split Values, demarcates the data, which is divided by commas in another file format. The XLSB extensions are used for a variety of tasks such as compression, storing, and opening. By selecting File > Save As from the Excel menu bar, you can save an Excel file in a different file format. There are a variety of file formats accessible in the Save As dialogue box, depending on what kind of sheet is active in the document; a single worksheet, chart worksheets, or another type of worksheet.

Format	Extension	Clipboard type identifiers
Picture	.wmf or .emf	Pictures in Windows Metafile Format (WMF) or Windows Enhanced Metafile Format (EMF). **Note** If you copy a Windows metafile picture from another program, Excel pastes the picture as an enhanced metafile.
Bitmap	.bmp	Pictures stored in Bitmap format (BMP).
Microsoft Excel file formats	.xls	Binary file formats for Excel versions 5.0/95 (BIFF5), Excel 97-2003 (BIFF8), and Excel 2010 (BIFF12).
SYLK	.slk	Symbolic Link Format.
DIF	.dif	Data Interchange Format.
Text (tab-delimited)	.txt	Tab-separated text format.
CSV (Comma-delimited)	.csv	Comma-separated values format.
Formatted text (Space-delimited)	.rtf	Rich Text Format (RTF). Only from Excel.
Embedded object	.gif, .jpg, .doc, .xls, or .bmp	Microsoft Excel objects, objects from properly registered programs that support OLE 2.0 (OwnerLink), and Picture or another presentation format.
Linked object	.gif, .jpg, .doc, .xls, or .bmp	OwnerLink, ObjectLink, Link, Picture, or other format.
Office drawing object	.emf	Office drawing object format or Picture (Windows enhanced metafile format, EMF).
Text	.txt	Display Text, OEM Text.
Single File Web Page	.mht, .mhtml	Single File Web Page (MHT or MHTML). This file format integrates inline graphics, applets, linked documents, and other supporting items referenced in the document. **Note:** This format is not supported in Excel 2007.
Web Page	.htm, .html	Hypertext Markup Language (HTML). **Note:** When you copy text from another program, Excel pastes the text in HTML format, regardless of the format of the original text.

For files that were generated in a previous version of Excel or another software but are not yet in the current file format, choose File > Open from the menu bar.

In Compatibility Mode, when you access an Excel 97-2022 workbook, the workbook immediately opens. Using the Excel 2022 file format will allow you to make use of the additional capabilities that have been added to the program since its release.

You do, however, have the option of continuing to work in Compatibility Mode, which keeps the original file format for older systems.

Chapter 3: The Excel Interface

The ribbon, which is a strip of controls that runs across the top area of the program window, serves as the focal point of the Excel interface. To locate tools, the ribbon is divided into tabs, each of which has a collection of controls. This nomenclature is used to designate the position of the various tools. For example, the Home page, Font grouping, and Bold button may be used to apply a bold font to a range of text that has been chosen. Following is a screenshot of the Microsoft Excel 2022 dialogue box with the Main screen selected and a workbook open with one blank worksheet:

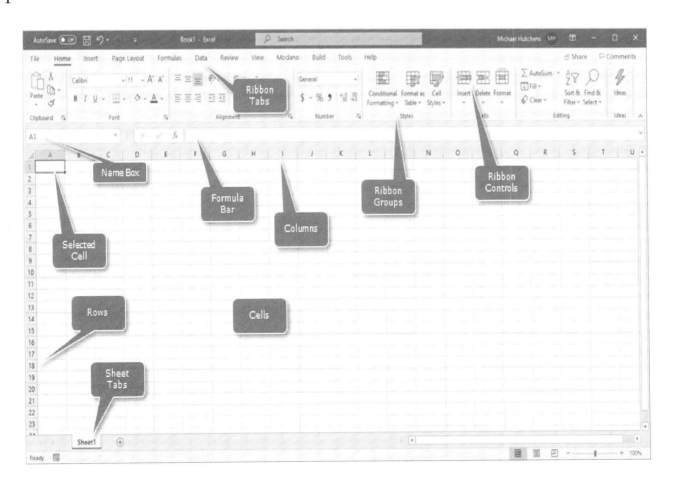

3.1 Understanding the Excel Interface

In this section, we will discuss Excel Interface.

Introducing the Concept of File Formats

An Excel workbook may be stored in a variety of formats, each of which has its own file extension, such as.xlsx or.xlsm, for example.

To create a new workbook in a certain format or to convert an old workbook in multiple formats, click on the File tab in the upper left corner of the screen and then pick the template sites from the Save As option that appears. If you prefer, you may use the key combination Alt+F+A to bring up the Save As dialogue box and then choose the appropriate file format in the Save As Type drop-down box.

Comparing and contrasting file formats

Each Excel file format has a varying amount of capability and compatibility with various versions of Excel, and this is reflected in the name of the format. When selecting a file format, it is important to keep this in mind. You should be aware that when you save an xlsm, xlsb, or another macro-enabled file as an an.xlsx file, all the macros in the original file will be deleted from the new file unless you specify otherwise.

The image below compares and contrasts the most regularly used Excel file formats, which are:

File Format	Extension	Compatibility	Functionality
Excel Workbook	.xlsx	Excel 2007 +	Standard file format with macros disabled.
Excel Macro-Enabled workbook	.xlsm	Excel 2007 +	Standard file format with macros enabled.
Excel Binary Workbook	.xlsb	Excel 2007 +	Compressed file format with macros enabled.
Excel 97-2003 Workbook	.xls	Excel 97 +	Standard Excel 97 -2003 file format with macros enabled.
CSV (Comma delimited)	.csv	Excel 97 +	Stores tabular data in plain-text form, separated by a comma.

Changing the Content of a Cell

A constant may be included in each cell of a worksheet. The word "constants" should be used instead of "hard-codes" or "inputs", since this is the most accurate and least confusing language. Examples of constant and formula cell contents are presented in the next section, with the formula bar indicating the contents of each cell.

Cell content can always be added and modified in the toolbar by entering or modifying the text in the formula bar and hitting Enter after each entry or modification. In some cases, this is referred to as "entering" data, but the accurate and least confusing reference is "inputting".

If you look at the formula instance in cell A3 above, you can make a reference to cell A2 by first entering '=' and then typing 'A2' or clicking on cell A2 with the mouse.

Formula Edit Mode is also shown in the example. During the data entering process, Excel enters Formula Edit Mode, which facilitates the entry of formulae by temporarily covering preceding ranges with colored boxes while the data is being entered, as you can see for cell A2 in this instance. To enter Formula, Modify Mode, pick the cell you want to edit and either start typing or use the F2 key to bring up the Formula Editor window.

3.2 Identification of The Screen Parts

The following are the ways to identify screen parts:

Toolbar with quick access buttons

By default, the Quick Access Toolbar (QAT) has buttons for saving, undoing, and redoing actions. You may, however, tailor the toolbar to your own requirements by clicking the buttons at the end of the bar and adding your own, or by right-clicking any icon on a tab and choosing Add to Quick Access Toolbar from the context menu that appears. To eliminate a button from your QAT Toolbar, just right-click on it and choose Delete from Quick Access Toolbar from the context menu that appears.

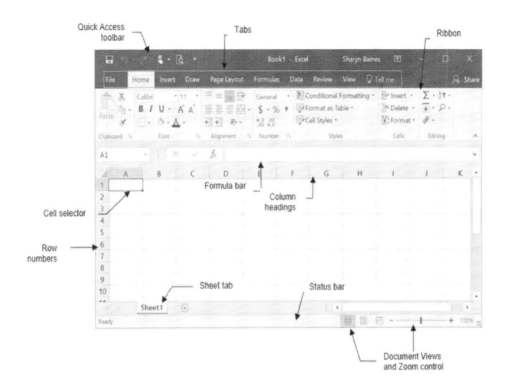

Tabs

Command keys are arranged into tabs for convenience. Those commands which are used for storing, printing, and transferring files are all found under the File tab. Among the most often used command options for altering and editing your worksheet are those found on the Home tab.

Ribbon

Every command key is included inside the Ribbon, which is located on each tab. It is possible that you will not require all of the instructions on a Ribbon. You will begin to recognize that you are simply using what you need. In addition, if you choose, you may include them in the QAT Toolbar as well.

Table headers, row numbers, and cell addresses.

Each column is identified by a phonetic alphabet, which is represented by the header bar. The Row number bar is located on the left-hand side of the screen, and it is used to identify each row with a unique number. A cell is defined as the point at which a column and a row cross. For example, the first cell in row 1 of column A is referred to as cell A1. Cell B3 is located on the third row of column B, and so on.

Choose a cell with the cell selection.

The cell selection is represented as a heavily outlined rectangle that represents the current working place in the document. Using the left mouse button to select a cell and the arrow keys to move the cell pointer are both acceptable methods of repositioning it. By dragging the mouse cursor over the selection, the cell pointer may be expanded to encompass several cells. If you look closely, you'll see that the row number and column letter "glow up" where the cell pointer is now located.

Formula bar

It is a tool that allows you to enter formulas into a program. The contents of the chosen cell are shown in the formula bar. If a calculation is included inside a cell, the formula bar will display the formula, while the particular cell in the grid region will display the result. To make changes to the contents of a cell, you may click inside the formula bar.

Tabs on a sheet

Sheet tabs (also known as worksheets) are also used to organize and analyze data in a spreadsheet. It is possible to create unique spreadsheets for each week of the year or for each employee, as an example. Whenever you develop a new worksheet (file) in Excel 2022, you will only be provided with one worksheet to work with. By selecting the Insert worksheet option, you may quickly and conveniently add to your existing worksheets.

The status bars

It displays current information. The information is shown in the Status bar changes based on what you are doing in the spreadsheet at the time. Example; If you have chosen several cells with values, the Status bar will display the total, average, and number of cells that have been selected in that row. In my essay "Find the Average, Count, and Total of a Range without Writing a Formula," I go into further detail on how to do this task.

Viewing the document and controlling the zoom level

To modify the layout or magnification of your screen, use the Documents view buttons as well as the Zoom control settings on your keyboard. If you are messing about with the view buttons, remember to always return to the Normal view to come back to Excel's default view when you are finished. Check out our entries on How to input information into an Excel worksheet, as well as Selecting cells and navigating around an Excel worksheet if you want to learn more about using the spreadsheet programs.

3.3 Title Bar

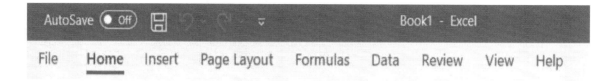

The title bar is a horizontal bar that appears at the top of a screen in a graphical user interface (GUI). It shows the title of the program, the name of the currently open document, and other information that identifies the contents of the window in which it is shown. Example; The title bar in the image below shows the program name "TextPad" and the file name "Document1" that is now being edited, but the rest of the window is blank.

3.4 Worksheet Tabs

When we open an excel workbook, we will see a row of rectangular tabs, each of which represents a different worksheet that can be edited. By default, there will be three spreadsheet tabs open, but we can add more tabs to the worksheet by clicking on the plus button provided at the end of each tab, and we can also rename or delete any of the spreadsheet tabs we have opened.

Worksheets serve as the foundation for the Excel program. These worksheets have their own tabs; every excel file must have at least one worksheet in it in order to function properly. We have a plethora of other things we can accomplish using the worksheet tab in Excel. This tab is located at the bottom of every worksheet in Excel.

3.5 Ribbon Tabs

The Excel Ribbon has nine tabs: File, Insert, Home, Page Layout, Data, Formulas, Review, View, and Help. When Excel first starts, the Home tab is selected as the default tab.

File

Creating a new spreadsheet, opening a document, saving the document, printing the document, and exporting a file are all available from the backstage view of this application.

Home

This section contains the most important or often used Excel commands, such as structuring, font types, and filtering, among others.

For example, the Clipboard group has instructions to cut, copy, and paste; and the Font group contains commands to change the font style, color, and size. Similar functions are categorized by group. Please keep in mind that your ribbon selections may display differently depending on the size of your screen and the size of your Excel session (when you shrink the size of your Spreadsheet window, you'll find that fewer buttons show).

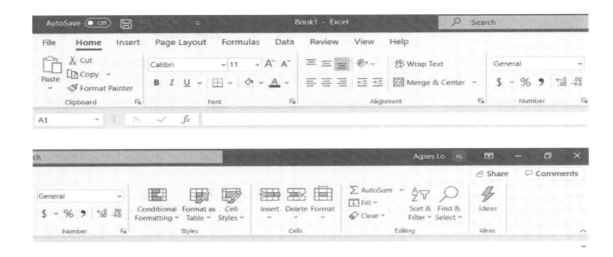

In order to provide you a better overview of all of the buttons & groups available, we have separated the page into two portions, as seen in the image above.

Insert

Here, users may insert a variety of different elements into a spreadsheet, such as Pivot Tables and photos and shapes, as well as charts, graphs, and symbols.

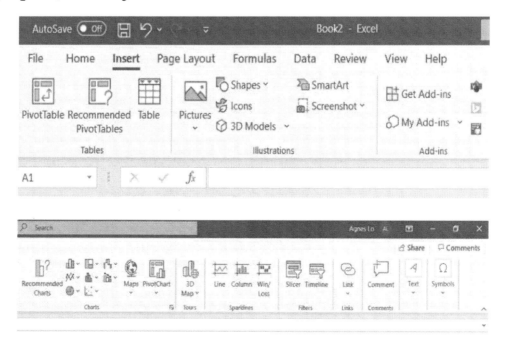

Page Layout

Users may personalize the style of the spreadsheet by modifying the margins, color themes, gridlines, and printing area, among other options. The modifications are also relevant when the document is printed.

Formulas

Here, all of the main formulae are organized into categories and made available via the function library, which also includes a variety of control settings.

Data

In addition to managing data inside the current spreadsheet, users may also import outside data from other sources into the file with this feature.

Review

Users may utilize this to do a variety of control operations, including spell check, translation, adding comments & notes, tracking changes, and enabling worksheet protection, among other things.

View

The worksheets may be viewed in a variety of ways, including with gridlines, zooming, freezing panes, and switching between windows.

Help

This provides access to Microsoft's technical help. It enables you to submit comments to the community as well as propose a feature to them.

3.6 What Is Spreadsheet?

Essentially, a spreadsheet in Microsoft Excel is a worksheet that has been split into multiple rows and columns to hold data relating to company inventory, revenue and costs, debts, and credit card balances, among other things. Electronic spreadsheets have supplanted the obsolete paper-based worksheets in the corporate sector of the modern-day.

A Microsoft Excel spreadsheet is made up of three components: rows, columns, and the intersections of these columns and rows, which are known as cells. In most cases, column labels are letters (A, B, C, D,), and row labels are numbers (1, 2, 3, 4,) to distinguish them from one another. In an MS Excel spreadsheet, a cell is formed by the intersection of two columns and two rows.

Every cell has been allocated an address, which includes the column name and row number of the cell. Keep in mind that the column letter will appear first, and the row number will come second in the address of a cell. An Excel 2022 file contains more than 18 billion cells, making it the largest spreadsheet ever created.

3.7 What Is a Cell?

Generally speaking, a cell is a rectangle space generated by the junction of two columns and two rows. Identifiers for cells include the Cell Name (or Reference, that may be derived by mixing the Column Letter only with Row Number) and the Row Number. In Row 3, for example, the cell in Column "C" would be designated as cell C3. Labels, numbers, formulas, and functions are all possible in a cell.

Cell Name

By default, the cell reference is the name of the cell in question. You may, however, use an alternate name to designate a specific cell or group of cells in your spreadsheet. After that, the alternative name may be utilized in formulae and functions to give a rapid means of jumping to a certain portion of the spreadsheet.

Cell Reference

It is the identifier of the cell that may be discovered by merging the Column Letter and the Row Number into a single string of characters. In Row 3, for example, the cell in Column's "C" would be designated as cell C3.

Column

On the spreadsheet screen, the columns are organized vertically. There are 256 columns in an Excel spreadsheet, and each column is labeled with a letter from the alphabet. The letter "Z" is reached by the column labels, which then go to the letters "AA," "AC," "AB," "AD," and "BC," "BA," "BB," "BD," and so on.

3.8 What Is a Row?

In the grid arrangement of a worksheet in MS Excel, a row is a horizontal line that goes across the page. In the horizontal rows, numeric numbers, such as 1, 2, and 3, are used to identify them. Vertical columns are labeled with alphabetical values such as A, B, and C to distinguish them from one another.

In the worksheet, each row has a unique row number, which can be referenced as a component of a cell reference, such as A2, A1, or M16, for example. By tapping on the row header, you may pick a whole row of data. In the above example, we have chosen row number 3. In Excel, you may perform a variety of things with rows, including inserting, removing, covering, unhiding, and resizing rows, as well as filters and conditional formatting.

3.9 What Is a Column?

Identifiable alphabetical header letters are used to signify and identify each column on the worksheet, which is situated at the top of the page. Excel spreadsheets may contain a total of 16,384 columns. Therefore, the column headings are labeled from A to XFD.

Columns are arranged vertically in the spreadsheet, and data is shown from top to bottom.

Chapter 4: Way to Use Excel Properly

Getting sense out of large volumes of data is made possible by Excel, which is an extremely powerful tool. However, it also performs well when doing basic computations, keeping track, and almost any kind of knowledge. It is the matrix of cells that holds the key to unleashing all of this potential. Cells may include any combination of numbers, text, and formulae. You enter information into your cells and arrange it in rows or columns. This enables you to add up your data, sort and classify it, organize it in tables, and create visually appealing charts and graphs. We will start by going over the fundamentals of how to use this site.

4.1 Opening A Spreadsheet

You can access a workbook by locating it on your desktop and double-clicking on it, but you can also open a file directly from inside the Excel software.

1. Select the File tab from the drop-down menu.
2. To open the file, click the Open button.
3. To rapidly show the Open tab in the Backstage view, use the Ctrl + O keyboard shortcut.
4. Choose the place in which the file will be stored.

You have a choice between the following:

- Recent; These are the most recent files you've edited on.

- Files that have been published with you about OneDrive and SharePoint Online are referred to as "Shared with Me".

- OneDrive is a cloud-based storage service provided by Microsoft.

- Your particular PC; Navigate through the files on your computer system. Navigate; This command opens a dialogue window in which you may browse through the folders, discs, and network shares on your machine.

- Choose the file that you wish to open.

- To open the file, click the Open button.

4.2 Working With The Ribbon

The Ribbon provides a variety of display choices to accommodate your tastes. However, a careless click might result in the Ribbon being mistakenly hidden.

To rapidly display the Ribbon, choose any tab on the toolbar, such as the Home and Insert tabs.

When you want the Ribbon to be visible at all times, click the arrow in the bottom part of the Ribbon.

You may modify your perspective of the Ribbon and maximize it by selecting Ribbon Display Options from the Ribbon drop-down menu at the top of your Excel page.

4.3 Managing Your Sheets

- From the window, you may switch between all of the worksheets.

- Drag and drop a worksheet from one Excel file to another, by simply clicking it on the window.

- All worksheets in an Excel workbook should be alphabetized.

- The context menu offers a plethora of additional choices for working with your worksheets.

- Find the sheet you're looking for quickly and easily across all your Excel files.

4.4 Entering Data

- Select the worksheets into which you will be inputting information.

- You may insert data into a cell or a range of cells by selecting the specific cell or group of cells you wish to use.

- In the first chosen cell, enter or change the information you wish to be shown.

- To return to its original screen, press TAB or ENTER on your keyboard.

To reject a selection of numerous sheets, pick any sheet that is not currently chosen. If there are no unselected sheets shown, right-click on the tab of a selected sheet and select Ungroup Pages from the menu bar.

Chapter 5: Formulas in Microsoft Excel

For novices who want to become effective in financial analysis, mastering the fundamental Excel formulae is essential. Data analysis software such as Microsoft Excel is largely viewed as the industry benchmark in this field. Additionally, Microsoft's spreadsheet application happens to be one of the most popular programs used by financial analysts, investment bankers, and other professionals in the fields of data processing, financial modeling, and presentation.

5.1 What Is Microsoft Excel Formulas?

Excel's fundamental terms are Formulas, and Functions; the two most fundamental methods to conduct computations in Microsoft Excel.

Formulas.

In Microsoft Excel, a formula is an operation that acts on the values in a variety of cell types or a single cell and is called a formula expression. For example, the expression "=A2+A1+A4" finds the sum of the values in the range from cell A1 to cell A4.

Functions.

In Excel, functions are preset algorithms that can be used. In addition to removing the need for time-consuming manual entering of formulae, they also provide human-friendly names. As an illustration; =SUM

(A2:A3). The procedure adds up all of the entries from A2 to A3, beginning with A1.

5.2 How to Insert Formulas in Microsoft Excel

Inserting Data into Excel can be done in five ways that save time. Obviously, each technique has its own set of benefits. As a result, before moving on to the core formulae, we'll go through those approaches in more detail so that you may start creating your preferred workflow as soon as possible.

1. Straightforward insertion: Entering a formula into the cell

Basic Excel formulae may be entered directly into a cell or the equation bar, which is the easiest way to enter them. Typically, the procedure begins with typing an equal sign, accompanied by the identification of a Microsoft Excel function.

When you begin entering the name of a function in Excel, a pop-up function suggestion will appear. This is a sophisticated feature of Excel. It is from this list that you will choose your preferred option. However, you should refrain from pressing the Enter key. As an alternative, tap the Tab key so that you may proceed to input further alternatives. Otherwise, you may see an incorrect name error, often shown as "#NAME?". Selecting the cell again and using the formula bar to finish your function will solve this problem.

2. Making use of the Insert Function option on the Formulas Tab.

If you want complete control over the insertion of functions into your spreadsheets, the Excel Insert Function modal dialog is all you'll ever need. Navigate to the Formulas tab and pick the first menu item labeled Insert Function from the drop-down menu. All of the capabilities you need to conduct your financial analysis in one convenient place; the dialogue box.

3. In the Formula Tab, choose a formula from one of the groups available.

This choice is for individuals who want to get to the heart of their favorite features as fast as possible. To access this option, browse the Formulas tab and choose the group that interests you. To display a sub-menu with a range of functions, choose Show Sub-Menu. You may then choose your preferred option from the drop-down menu. If, on the other hand, you discover that your selected group is not listed on the tab, tap on the More Features option—it's most likely tucked away there.

4. Making Use of the AutoSum Option

The AutoSum method is the go-to solution for fast and daily calculations. Head to the Home tab and choose the AutoSum option in the far-right corner of the screen. Then click on the caret to see any further hidden formulae. This choice is also accessible on the Formulas tab, where it appears as the second choice after the Add

Function.

5. Quick Insert: Make use of tabs that have been recently used.

It is possible to save time by using the Recently Used option instead of having to type your most recent equation again. It's located on the Formulas tab, the third menu item on the left-hand side of the screen, right next to AutoSum.

5.3 How to Use Most Common Microsoft Excel Formulas

For your Workflow, here are seven common Excel Formulas to know. We'll begin with some essential Excel functions to get you started because you've now mastered the ability to input your favorite formulae and have them operate properly.

1. SUM

The SUM formulae are the first calculation in Excel that every user should be familiar with. Most of the time, it combines values from a choice of rows or columns inside the range you've specified.

=SUM (number3, [number4],) is the sum of the first and second numbers.

Example:

=SUM (B3:G3) – This straightforward selection sums up the amount in a row.

=SUM (A4:A8) – This straightforward selection combines the values in a single column.

=SUM (A2:A8)/20 – This demonstrates that you can convert your function into a formula.

2. The Median

You should be reminded of basic averages of data, such as the mean stockholders in a certain shareholding pool while using the AVERAGE function.

=AVERAGE (number1, [number2],) is a mathematical expression.

Using the following example, we can see a basic average, which is similarly comparable to (SUM (B2:B11)/10).

3. Compare And Differentiate

The COUNT function tallies the number of cells in a certain range that contains solely numeric values, as specified by the argument.

=COUNT (value1, [value2],) =COUNT (value1, [value2],)

Example:

COUNT (A: A) — This function counts the number of numerical values in the A column. To count rows, you must, however, modify the range included inside the formula.

COUNT (A1:C1) – It may now count the number of rows.

COUNTA is the fourth item on the list.

COUNTA is similar to the COUNT function in that it counts all cells in a particular range. However, it counts all cells, regardless of their kind. As opposed to the numeric-only COUNT function, which counts only dates and times, string-valued logical values, errors, an empty string, and text-valued logical values.

=COUNTA (value1, [value2],) =COUNTA (value1, [value2],) =COUNTA (value1, [value2],)

Example:

COUNTA (C2:C13) – Counts the number of rows in column C from 2 to 13, regardless of the type. To count rows, you cannot, however, use the same algorithm as you would for COUNT. You must make an adjustment to the selection within the brackets—for example, COUNTA (C1:H3) will count columns C to H. COUNTA (C1:H3) will count columns C to H.

5. IF Function

This function is frequently employed when it is necessary to sort data following predetermined logic. The most advantageous feature of the IF formula is that it allows you to incorporate formulae and functions inside it.

=IF (logical test, [value if true], [value if false]) is a conditional expression.

Example; =IF (C2D3, 'TRUE,' 'FALSE') – Determines if the value at C2 is smaller than the value at D3 by comparing the two. If the reasoning is correct, the cell value should be TRUE; otherwise, it should be FALSE.

6. Trim

The TRIM function ensures that your routines do not produce errors due to disorderly spaces in their input. In this way, it guarantees that all vacant spots are removed. In contrast to other functions, TRIM can only work on a single cell instead of other functions that can act on a range of cells. As a result, it has the disadvantage of introducing redundant data into your spreadsheet.

=TRIM (text)

Example:

TRIM(A2) — This function removes any blank spaces from the value in cell A2.

7. Maximum And Minimum

The MAX & MIN functions are useful for determining the maximum and least numbers in a value range that may be found.

=MIN (number1, [number2],) =MIN (number1, [number2],)

Example;

=MIN (B2:C13) – Finds the smallest number between column B from

B2 and column C from C2 to row 13 in both columns B and C. =MIN (B2:C11) – Finds the smallest number between column B from B2 and column C from C2 to row 11.

=MAX (number1, [number2],) is a mathematical formula.

Chapter 6: Functions in Excel

A new generation of functions has evolved to carry out the functional obligations of any program, and they are particularly crucial in Excel. It saves time by removing the need to undertake extensive computations for each research or query that needs answers based on a future period or event. Functional formulae are well-established formulas that carry out computations by mixing certain numbers (arguments) in a predetermined sequence (syntax). For example, the SUM function may sum values or cell groups together. Consider the following scenario; you wish to insert a list of 100 numbers into a column, beginning at column A1 and finishing at cell A100. Even if you desired to, you wouldn't be allowed to insert 100 distinct additions in a single cell because then you'd run out of room before you could finish.

Another way, a function = SUM may be entered (A1:A100). As a result, given the parameters A9, A5, A7, and A100, the summation function returns the total of 100 values multiplied together. Several other arguments may be used, including integers, text, logical values such as True or Untrue, arrays, error values (such as #N/A), and cell references. To provide an argument, you must supply an argument that yields a rational number for the argument you are specifying. Constants, formulas, and other functions may all be used as arguments, as can other data types.

6.1 The Importance Of Functions

A function is a predetermined formula that uses particular values in a specific order. A function can be defined as follows; one of the most significant advantages of functions is that they may save you time by eliminating the need to create the formula from scratch. Excel has thousands of functions that may be used to aid you with your computations. It is critical to consider the sequence in which you introduce functions. Each function has a precise sequence that must be given the opportunity for the procedure to perform effectively. This order is referred to as syntax. A formula containing a function is created by inserting an equal's sign (=), the function name (for example, the function SUM is the name for addition), and an argument into a formula expression. These are the pieces of information that will be used to calculate the formula, such as a variety of cell references.

6.2 The Parts of a Function

A function should be written in a precise form to operate properly; this is referred to as syntax. The fundamental grammar of a function comprises the equals sign (=), the functional name (for example, SUM), and one or more parameters. The information you wish to compute is included inside the arguments. The method in the following example combines the values from cells A1 through A20.

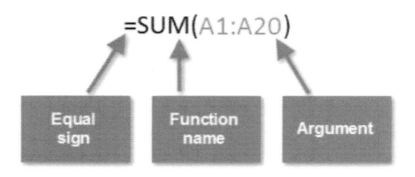

6.3 Advanced Functions

Excel provides a plethora of useful functions and uses. The most common form is used by 95% of the users. Advanced Excel formulas and functions are available to help you with more sophisticated computations in Excel. In contrast to the advanced Excel formula, which is used to extract new information from a specific data group, the functions are intended for quick search and formatting of a vast pool of data.

VLOOKUP

Using the function, you may search for a certain set of information in a vast data section and then extract that information into your freshly created table. It is necessary to go to the function choice. You may type 'VLOOKUP' into the insert function tab, or you can choose it from the drop-down selection. Following the selection of this option, a wizard's box will pop up, displaying a new set of box possibilities.

Addition and Subtraction Functions

This feature is most commonly used to add a collection of figures in a single column. Following the selection of a portion of the column, the calculator has a single button in the Tab which can be used.

The MAX MIN function

This method is used to extract the maximum and lowest values from a collection of data that has been chosen at random. To ensure the highest value, you must enter 'MAX' in the function tab and to obtain the minimum value, you must enter 'MIN' in the function tab. The values will be drawn from the main data table by the function on its initiative.

IF Conditional Expression

The IF statement is used to extract true and false information about a parameter that has been entered into the variables box. The IF statement may be written or split down as follows:

IF

Values for the criteria are: (True, False)

Following the criteria placement in the chosen column, the responses are utilized to verify the prediction and provide outcomes following the forecast.

The SUMIF Function

The SUMIF function allows you to search for a specific collection of information that satisfies your requirements by using a formula. It is necessary to input the criteria in a wizard's box that comprises three tabs: the range, criteria, and sum limit. The range tab denotes the region in which you wish to conduct your search. The criterion tab locates the cell in question, and the total range tab sums up all the data that meets your requirements.

IN ADDITION, Function

This feature is used to specify more than one search criterion for the variables to be searched. If the variable meets the numerous criteria, the value is reported as True; otherwise, the search returns FALSE. The wizard box is divided into tabs, each of which allows you to input a logical list of conditions to determine the behavior of a particular collection of data. On the right of the screen, another column has the words TRUE and FALSE.

OR Function

The OR operation is a bit different from the AND function that came before it. In contrast to the AND function, the OR function looks for just one requirement to be TRUE, then pulls the value; in contrast, the AND function requires every criterion to match to provide a TRUE result. If none of the criteria are met, the LEFT Function returns the FALSE value. The LEFT function allows you to choose a portion of the data in a specified column from the left-hand side of the screen. Commands allow you to specify the variables or the amount of data you wish to store in your new column.

THE CORRECT FUNCTION

Using parameters in the command box, you may separate data from the chosen column set on the right-hand side of the screen display by setting them in the command box.

THE FUNCTION OF CONCATENATION

This function in Excel is a mix of the LEFT and RIGHT Functions, and it creates a new column of data by setting a variable to grab a certain chunk of the data from both the left and right sides of the worksheet.

The ROUND functions

This method is used to round up data with a large number of digits just after the decimal place to make calculations more convenient. This cell does not need any formatting.

PROPER function

It is necessary to utilize this correct function to capitalize or capitalize the characters of a phrase inside the cells. It is possible to complete this in a customized manner. You can modify the letters in any format you like on a per-letter basis.

6.4 Working with Arguments

Arguments may refer to single cells and cell ranges, but they must be placed inside parenthesis to be effective. According to the syntax needed by the function, you may provide a single parameter or many arguments.

Example; The function =MEAN (B1:B9) will compute the arithmetic mean in the selected cell M1:M9 using the data in the first nine cells of the array. This function takes a single parameter and returns a value.

6.5 Creating Function

To create a basic function in Excel:

- Choose the cell where the answer will be displayed (F15, for example).
- Type the equals symbol (=), followed by the function's name (SUM, for example).
- Within the parentheses, enter the cells used for the argument.
- Hit Enter and the answer will show on the screen.

Unit Price		Ordered	Date Received
$12.03		18-Sep	26-Sep
$15.95		18-Sep	26-Sep
$5.87		8-Aug	14-Aug
$8.83		8-Aug	14-Aug
$13.54	$27.08	22-Jul	29-Jul

6.6 How to Enter a Function Manually

In Excel, you may create a function manually. The following are the steps:

1. To insert a formula into a cell, select it and press Enter.
2. To insert a function, use the Insert Function icon.
3. The following method is one that can look for a function; Type a few terms that define the function you're looking for and hit the Go button.
4. Select the required function from the drop-down menu.
5. To proceed, click OK...
6. Fill in the blanks with the formula arguments.
7. To proceed, click OK.

6.7 The Function Library

Just a few of the hundreds of functions available in Microsoft Excel will be appropriate for the sort of data you're dealing with. Even though you are not required to master every single function, you may choose to become acquainted with some of the various kinds to understand which ones could be useful to you as you develop new spreadsheets. The Function Library, which can be found on the Formulas page, is a fantastic resource for learning about functions. From this menu bar, you may search and pick Excel functions classification such as Economic, Analytic, Linguistic, and Date & Time.

- Choose the cell where the answer will be displayed (I6, for example).
- Select the Formulas tab from the drop-down menu.
- Choose the function category you need from the Function Library grouping in the left-hand navigation bar. In this instance, we'll use the Date and Time fields.
- First, choose the function you want to perform from the Date and-or Time drop-down box. In our worksheet, we'll use the NETWORKDAYS method to count the number of days between the purchase date and the delivery date.
- The Function Arguments dialogue box will be shown after that. Insert the mouse in the first column, then input or pick the cell(s) you wish to work with from the drop-down menu (G6, for example).

- Insert the pointer in the text field, and then enter or choose the cell(s) you wish to edit in the next field (H6, for example).

- After you click OK, the outcome will be shown. According to our findings, it spent 5 days getting the order from the supplier.

6.8 Insert Function Command

A useful feature of the Insert Function is that it enables you to look for a function by giving a summary of what you're searching for or by choosing a category to browse through. The Insert Function option may also be used to input or pick more than one parameter for a function, which is very convenient.

In this example, our goal is to select and implement a method that will calculate the total amount of supplies reported in the Office Orders Log. The normal COUNT function only numbers cells containing numbers; however, we want to count the columns in the Office Supply columns with text instead of numbers. Therefore, we'll have to develop a formula that shows the number of cells that contain text.

- Choose the cell where the answer will be displayed (A27, for example).

- Choose the Insert Function from the Formulas tab, which can be found on the Formulas tab.

- Fill in the blanks with a summary of the function you're looking for, and then press Go. You can also explore by choosing a category from the drop-down menu.

- Examine the findings to determine which function you need (COUNTA, for example). To proceed, click OK.

- The Function Arguments dialogue box will be shown after that. Insert the mouse in the first column, then input or pick the cell(s) you wish to work with from the drop-down menu (A6:A14, for example).

- Insert the mouse pointer in the text field, and then insert or choose the cell(s) you want to edit in the following field (A19:A23, for example). If necessary, you may continue to add more reasons to your argument.

- After you click OK, the outcome will be shown. According to our findings, 14 Total Items were purchased from our log.

Chapter 7: Excel Tricks and Keyboard Shortcuts

This chapter primarily comprehends the notion of certain uncommon tricks and other functions, which will be discussed later. These two portions of the chapter are divided into two parts: the first exposes you to keyboard shortcuts, then the second covers the many office elements associated with Excel. After finishing this section, you will be capable of completing the following tasks:

Using the shortcut keyboard to speed up the process. The components of Excel that were installed are listed below. As we learned in the last section on Excel, shortcut keys have always been the most effective technique. The term "shortcut" refers to the ability to do a job at the smallest level of effort. However, although it is advised that you follow the menu or mouse directions to the point, it is strongly urged that you finish the operation using shortcut keys to save time and increase productivity instead. Please study the following topics associated with shortcut keys; we are convinced that you will discover the best answer and increase your training by at least 30% in your typical curriculum. The key sequence is purely to instruct you on which key sequence works in a different mode to complete the job at hand.

7.1 Useful Tricks That Make Excel Easy

Key Combination is following:

- These keys are used to move around and scroll through a worksheet or workbook.
- Control keys for previewing & printing a document.
- Function keys for dealing with worksheets.
- Charts and macros are included.

The arrow keys are used to navigate.

One cell may be dragged down, up, left, or right in any direction.

Using the arrow keys and the CTRL key, navigate to the extreme edge of the currently displayed data area.

Home

To return to the beginning of the row, press [Enter].

CTRL+HOME

To return to the beginning of the worksheet, click here.

CTRL+END

Navigate to the final cells on the worksheet, which is typically A1 and is placed at the junction of the rightmost used column and the bottom-most used row (in the lower right corner) of the worksheet.

PAGE DOWN

Go down one screen to the next one.

PAGE UP

Enlarge the screen resolution on your computer.

ALT+PAGE DOWN is a keyboard shortcut.

Drag one panel to the right by right-clicking and dragging it.

7.2 Keyboard Shortcuts for Microsoft Excel

Excel has several function keys that may help you work more quickly and effectively while increasing your productivity. Instead of using the mouse to reach the toolbar, just 2 - 3 keystrokes are required to execute most major activities. Isn't that a lot more convenient and timesaving?

The next issue is whether or not you must remember these shortcuts, and the answer is no. It would be advantageous, though, if you could recall a couple of them from memory. Most standard Excel shortcuts will become second nature, with a little consistent practice and repetition.

Key Sequence Required	Function
CTRL+P or CTRL+SHIFT+F12	The Print dialogue box will appear.
Arrow Keys	Move around the page when zoomed in.
PAGE UP or DOWN	Move by one page when zoomed out.
CTRL+UP ARROW or	Move to the first page when zoomed out
CTRL+LEFT ARROW	
CTRL+DOWN ARROW or CTRL+RIGHT ARROW	Move to the last page when zoomed out
CTRL+F11 or ALT+SHIFT+F1	Add a new worksheet.
F11 or ALT+F1	Make a chart with the current range.
ALT+F8	The Macro dialogue box will appear.
ALT+F11	The Visual Basic Editor will appear.
CTRL+F11	Create a macro sheet in Microsoft Excel 4.0.

Chapter 8: Analyzing Data in Excel

This section demonstrates some of the great tools Excel has to provide for data analysis.

1. The first sorting option is to filter your Excel data by a column or many columns. You have the option of sorting in either ascending or descending.

2. When you wish to show just records that fulfill particular criteria, you may filter your Excel files using the Filter function.

3. The third feature is conditional formatting, which allows you to emphasize cells with a specific color based on the cell's value.

4. Diagrams; a simple Excel diagram may convey more information than a statistics page. As you will see, producing charts is a simple process.

5. Pivot Tables; tables are among the most powerful capabilities that Excel offers. Using a pivot table, it is possible to derive statistical significance from a big, comprehensive data collection.

6. Master Excel tables to evaluate your data streamlined and straightforwardly with these six tips.

7. What-If Analysis: What-If Assessment in Excel enables you to experiment with alternative values (scenarios) for formulae by modifying the formulas.

In addition to the other tools in Excel, there is a solver that applies operations research principles to identify optimum solutions for a variety of decision issues.

8.1 Make Pivot Table

In Excel, a Pivot Table is an active table that can synthesize large quantities of data in a short period. Using various pages, you may filter the data by rotating the rows and columns, and you can explore information for certain regions of interest by rotating the rows and columns. The accompanying information is mainly intended to assist you in understanding the idea, purpose, and other connected features of the subject matter included in this section.

When and why would a Pivot Table be used?

The use of a Pivot Table report is helpful when you need to analyze related totals. This is particularly true when you have a large list of data to summarize and compare multiple details about each figure. Whenever you need Microsoft Excel to handle the sorting, subtotaling, and totaling, Pivot Table reports are the best option. Because a Pivot Table is interactive, you or other users may alter how the data is shown.

To create a PivotTable report, you must first create a PivotTable. Use the PivotTable or PivotChart Wizards as a guide to locate and identify the source data you desire to analyze and create the standard format for a PivotTable report, among other things. It is then possible to utilize the Pivot Table toolbar to organize the data inside the framework created.

This section will discuss the many types of PivotTable reports. The following are examples of a normal Pivot Table report. Indented PivotTable reports allow you to see all of the summary statistics of the same kind in a single column by showing the report in indented style. Create a PivotChart report to view the data in graphical form. Anyone who has access to a PivotTable list on a Website page may read and interact with the data in an Excel PivotTable report published to a PivotTable list on a New website. PivotTable reports may be prepared using an Excel Spreadsheets list, Excel worksheets from an external system, or data from another PivotTable report as the source data. The following source data is used for the remainder of the sample reports on this subject to allow for comparisons between the considerable variation of the same data.

Instructions on how to set up the data source

Organizing data from Excel lists and most datasets are accomplished via rows and columns. Your source data must include similar facts and appear in the same column. As shown in the example, the area for purchase is always in column E, and the amount sold is always in column D, and so on.

OLAP data source information

Rather than storing data in rows and columns, OLAP databases aggregate amounts of information into aspects and levels. Because the overview statistics for the PivotTable are calculated by the OLAP server rather than by Excel, you may use PivotTable reports to present and analyze data from OLAP databases rather than Excel. A more efficient data retrieval method is provided by an OLAP database, which allows you to study bigger volumes of data than you'd get from other kinds of databases. Using Excel, you can also generate OLAP cubes from data in other databases and store them as cube files, allowing you to interact with them when not connected to the internet.

A PivotTable report's fields and items are defined as follows: Each field corresponds to a column in the data sources, and each item combines data sets from the source data. The fields of a PivotTable report list data items that are spread across rows or along columns. The cells at the convergence of the rows and columns offer a summary of the information for the objects at the top of the column and on the left side of the row at the intersection of the rows and columns.

PivotTable reports are derived from data fields, such as Sum of Sales, which give the values for summarization in the Pivot table.

Summary Operations: Pivot Table analyzes employ summary functions to summarize the values of data fields. These functions include sum, count, and average. If you want to show subtotals and grand totals, these functions will also automatically produce them for you. It is necessary to sum the data from the Sales column in the match to source to show subtotals for the months and grand tallies for the rows and columns in this example.

In most PivotTable reports, you may see the detail tables from the data sources that make up the aggregate value in a single data column, known as "seeing details". Although OLAP source data is not organized in rows that can be viewed in this fashion, if your PivotTable report is based on OLAP source data, you may alter the amount of information provided throughout the report.

Changing the layout: By moving a field button to a different section of the PivotTable, you may examine your data in various ways and produce various summary results. Rather than gazing along the rows, you can see the identities of salespeople across the columns, which saves you time and effort. You may change the layout of the report by sliding a field or item around.

The following are the elements of the PivotTable report: The indented structure of a Pivot Table is similar to the format of a regular database banding report or produced report, with the exception of the number of columns. The data for each row field is recessed in a manner similar to that of a text outline. This style allows you to view all the aggregated figures for a data field in a single column by utilizing a single column. It's especially useful for long reports or reports that must be printed out in full.

Visualizations of PivotTable Data tables: A PivotChart, like a PivotTable, is an interactive graph that allows you to observe and rearrange data visually. PivotTable reports are always included with PivotChart reports in the same worksheet, and they include all the source data for the reports they are connected with. As with a PivotTable report, field buttons are included in a PivotChart report, which you can use to customize the layout and show different types of data.

When using PivotTables on the web, it is possible to save a PivotTable report as a Web page that can subsequently be published to a public site, such as a Web server. Its report version is called a PivotTable list, and it has many of the same interactive elements as the report in Microsoft Excel, including pivot tables. Other users who have the Microsoft Office Web Technologies installed on their computers may see and interact with the PivotTable list by using the Microsoft Internet Explorer Web software version 4.01 or later.

Installing Office Web Components is as simple as installing Microsoft Office, or users may download Office Web Components from their company's intranet if their employer has an Office site license and wants to use them.

Row Fields: In a PivotTable, fields from the primary source data are assigned a row orientation based on their position in the table. Consider the following scenario as an illustration. Product and Sold By are two of the row fields. When there is more than one-row field in a

PivotTable report, the inner row field is the one that is closest to the data area. The outer row fields refer to any leftover row fields not included in this list. The medial and lateral row fields have differing qualities from one another. The items in the outermost field are only shown once; however, those in the remaining fields are displayed as many times as necessary.

Column Field: The term "Column Field" refers to a field that has a column orientation in a PivotTable. Consider the following scenario as an illustration. Within the Quarters column, there are two fields named Qtr2 and Qtr3. When creating a PivotTable report, it is possible to incorporate a number of important pieces of information. It can include column fields in the same way as it can have row fields. In most PivotTables with a nested structure, column fields are not accessible for selection.

Item

A PivotTable field's subclass or member is an item. Items in the source data correspond to distinct entries in the same field and column as those in the source data. Items are shown as row or column labels and drop-down menus for page field drop-downs.

Page Field

A page field is used to specify the alignment of a page or filter on a page or filtering system. In this example, the region field is a page field that you can use to filter the report by region if you choose. Using the

Region option, you may show summarized data for only the East region, West region, or all areas. Whenever you pick a special item in a page field, the PivotTable report changes to only display the summarized information related to selecting that item.

Each distinct entry or value from the field, or row, in the source list or table, for example, is designated as an item in the page field list. Page Field Item "The East" region has been chosen in the Area page field, and the PivotTable report only displays data for that region at the time of writing.

Data Field

A ground containing information from a source list or database will be summarized. For example, the term "Sum of Sales" refers to a data field that adds up the items in the Sales field or column of the source data. In the example of an indented-format report, this field is referred to as Sales rather than Sum of Sales. It is typical for data fields to include quantitative data, such as statistics or sales figures, but it is also possible to have text data. For summarizing text data in PivotTable reports, Microsoft Excel defaults to using the Count summary function and the Sum summary function when summarizing numeric data.

Data area

In a PivotTable report, this part contains summary data. All of the items in the rows or columns fields are consolidated into the cells of the data area. Each value in the data area is a condensed version of the information contained in the source records or rows.

On the right side of each field, a drop-down arrow allows you to choose a different option. By clicking on this arrow, you can choose which objects you want to display. In PivotTable reports built on source data from OLAP databases, the field arrow shows just the highest-level field in a dimension, and you may pick items at several levels in the field. When you choose a year from the drop-down arrow in the Year box, you may be presented with the following. When items in a field are selected, the Expand Indicator (or OR symbol) appears next to them. To reveal or conceal information for an item, select the item by clicking on its indication.

8.2 Analyzing Data Sets with Excel

Analyze Data has been updated to better reflect how ideas enable data analysis to be easier, quicker, and more intuitive. The function was formerly known as "Ideas". The user interface and functionality remain unchanged, and they continue to comply with the same safety and licensing rules. If you're on the Semi-Annual Corporate Channel, you may even see "Suggestions" until Excel has been updated to reflect the change.

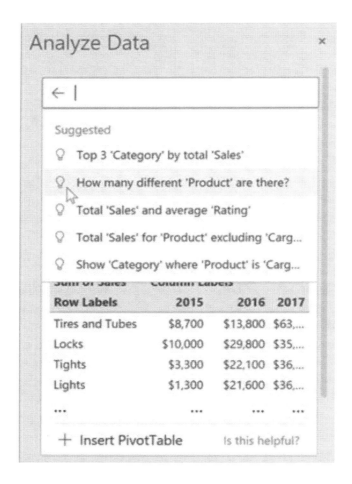

Analyzing Data in Excel gives you the ability to better understand your data by allowing you to ask questions about the data without having to create difficult algorithms. Natural language queries are used to aid this.

Apart from that, Analyze Data delivers high-level visual summaries, trends, and patterns of data. Simply choose a cell in a data range and then click on the Analyze Data icon on the Home tab to do the analysis. When you run Analyze Data in Excel, it will analyze your data and offer visually attractive results in a task window. Entering a topic in the query box that appears in the window and pressing Enter will provide more particular information if you are looking for it.

When Analyze Data is activated, it will give responses in visuals like tables, charts, and PivotTables, which can then be added to the worksheet. You may get customized recommended questions by choosing the query box in the Analyze Data window if you are interested in investigating your data or want to understand what is available.

8.3 Tips and Tricks

Here are some pointers on how to get the most out of Analyze Data:

1.   Analyze Data performs best when data is presented in the form of an Excel table. Select a cell in your dataset and hit the Ctrl+T keyboard shortcut to build an Excel table.

2.   Always make sure the columns have appropriate headings. Headers should consist of a single row of non-blank headers for each column distinct from the others. Avoid duplicate rows of headings, merged cells, and similar practices.

3.   Use Power Query to transform tables with a pass, or many rows of headers, if your data is difficult to understand or nested.

8.4 Data Visualization

The procedures needed to produce data visualizations in Excel depend on the kind of graphical display you pick to display the information. The approach for creating simple visuals is much the same as creating complex representations. More complicated datasets and illustrations may need the implementation of extra processes. To generate a data visualization in Excel, begin by organizing your data into a spreadsheet.

This should contain all of your labels, as well as the final dataset. Afterward, underline the information you want to include in your graphic, including the labels. Select "insert" from the main menu and afterward select the type of chart or graph you want to create from the drop-down menu. As soon as you've chosen, the visualization will display in your spreadsheet without your intervention. Use the right-click menu to make changes to the chart or graph's details, such as the name, axis labels, and colors. This will bring up a pop-up or side window with choices to add a legend, modify the scale, and change the font styles and sizes, among other things.

8.5 Data Reporting

To open a report in Microsoft Excel, go to Controllers > Report > Open Report. The report is now open. To run a report in Microsoft Excel, go to Controllers > Reporting > Run Report. Create a report. The window titled "Run Reports" appears. Fill the blanks with the reality, period, and anticipated actuality for which we wish the report to be generated. To produce a report for a certain consolidation type and firm, enter the information in the appropriate fields. The currency type you wish to produce the report should be entered in the appropriate field. This may be either the local currency (LC) or a converted currency based on the group's currency union in the firm structure, such as the LE currency in this case. Enter the denomination code you wish to use, for example, ER, in the appropriate field. It is only necessary to complete this area if you are producing a report that has multi-currency business codes ($M) as the currency type. The extended aspect for which you wish to produce the report should be entered here. If no dimensions are specified, the total value will be used instead. The closure version/journal type about which you wish to produce the report should be entered here. As a default, the REP symbol is utilized. Toggle between the Closing Version and the Journal Type by selecting the appropriate check box. The contribution version and automated journal type you wish to create the report should be entered in the appropriate fields. Toggle between the contribution version and the automated journal type by selecting the appropriate check box. Enter the accounts, the form, the movement extension, and the counter company in which you wish to produce a report into the appropriate fields. As soon as you click OK, the Excel file will grow to include rows and columns of information. Altering the report layout in Excel and entering Cognos Controllers Report methods or IBM Cognos Controllers Link for Excel Spreadsheets functions is now possible.

In Microsoft Excel, go to Controllers > Report > Save Report to save the report you created. It is converted to a Controller Link worksheet when you choose the Office Button or Save As option in Microsoft Excel 2007.

8.6 The Importance of Reporting All Results

There is a limit on how many reports may be generated at one time. In certain cases, you may not be able to select more than one period simultaneously. In order to do this, you must first produce the reports from Controller/Reports/Run.

When creating a report, the report's structure decides which parameters are relevant to the report. For example, if a certain business is specified in the column description of a report, choosing a different company at the time of Reports Run will have no impact on the report. Check out the Create Reports section for additional information on creating reports.

Please refer to the Cognos Controllers Functions tables for further information on how to insert functions and the parameters that go with them.

Chapter 9: Tables & Their Importance

A table is a useful method for managing and arranging data together in Excel. Define a table to be a distinct group of multiple rows and columns in a spreadsheet, contrasted to a list. You may have numerous tables on the same page if you want to be more organized.

Your data in a Spreadsheet may be already organized into a table since it's organized into rows and columns and is all in one place. However, unless you've utilized the special Excel data table function, your data isn't organized in a real "table" format.

To make it simpler to manage and analyze a set of linked data, you may create an Excel table from a variety of cells in your spreadsheet. Tables may be the most useful tool in Excel that you're not currently making use of. In Excel, creating a table is a simple process. A data table may be created from flat data in only a few clicks (or by using a single keyboard shortcut). This has a number of advantages over a flat data table.

There are several benefits to using an Excel table, including the following:

1.   Styles in a hurry. Add color, banded rows, or header styles with a single click to your data to make it more visually appealing.

2.   Table headings. Give tables a name so they can be referred to in other calculations more easily.

3.   Formulas that are less polluting. When working in a table, Excel formulas are considerably simpler to understand and write than when working in a spreadsheet.

4.   The auto-expand feature is enabled. In Excel, when you add a new row and column to your information, the table is instantly updated to accommodate the newly added cells.

5.   Filters and subtotals are included. As you filter your data, automatic filter icons and subtotals have added that change as you do.

9.1 Tables Types

In Excel, we can build three different sorts of tables. These are the ones:

A general Excel table, sometimes known as an "Excel Table"

If the rows or columns of the data are specified, a standard Excel table is a critical component for grouping the information. A single Excel worksheet page may include many tables, each of which can be referenced in formulae by their respective header titles. Data in Excel appears to be in a tabular form since information is collected in the grid format in the spreadsheet. However, by definition, it is not regarded as a table in Microsoft Excel. It is necessary to define a range of collections of cells as a table before they may be used.

Informational Table

The Data table is a very intriguing tool discovered in the What-If Research feature of Microsoft Excel, and is extremely easy to use. With the help of a data table, we may compute any argument that depends on a variety of factors. The formula is applied to a data table, and the value changes as a result of one or two aspects in the table being changed.

The PivotTable is the third item on the list.

The PivotTable is a particular Excel table tool that allows you to rearrange the columns and rows of a data collection in any way you like. In fact, this tool makes no modifications to the original data; instead, it changes the data direction and generates some unique outputs from the data. When dealing with a huge quantity of data, the PivotTable comes in handy. It saves us time by allowing us to calculate quickly. It can also execute various operations, such as sum, mean, sort, grouping, and count, among others.

9.2 How Can You Make a Table in Excel?

We'll go through the process of creating several types of Excel tables in this section. In this part, we'll go over how to make a generic Excel table, as well as its specific features, and its advantages and disadvantages, all with a full explanation.

How to Build an Excel Table in Microsoft Excel

To construct an Excel Table, follow the instructions outlined in this section:

1. To begin, choose any column or row in the database by clicking on it.
2. Then, choose the home option from the drop-down menu.
3. Then, using the Styles tool, pick the Style as a Table option.
4. Choose any of the predefined table styles.
5. Alternatively, we might use the keyboard shortcut Ctrl+T.

6. Create Table will be the name of the new dialogue box displayed.

7. If the data set has any headers, choose the My table includes headers checkbox.

8. Now, click on the OK button.

PivotTables: How to Create Them

To construct a PivotTable, go through the procedures outlined below:

1. To begin, choose the Insert tab from the toolbar.

2. Then, pick PivotTable from the drop-down menu.

3. Alternatively, select From Table/Range first from the drop-down menu.

4. Insert the Table Range & Table Location information.

5. Then click on the OK button.

6. Select items from the PivotTable Columns at this point.

7. As we can see, a Total row has been included. The numerous columns of the Table Format may be customized to our liking.

Data Table in Excel

This step will use the data table to apply to one variable alone. For this part, we are taking into consideration the number of EMI variables.

1. First, we create a column that has distinct EMI values.

2. The formula in the cell that includes the formula relates to the cell-on-Cell E5 in the worksheet.

3. Now, hit the Enter key on your keyboard.

4. Afterwards, choose the cells as indicated in the illustration below.

5. To begin, navigate to the Data tab.

6. Then, from the What-If Study menu, pick the Data Table option.

7. A new dialogue box will display. Click OK to dismiss it.

8. In the Columns input cells box, we prefer to refer to the column of the variables that have been applied in this instance of the program.

9. Then click on the OK button.

9.3 Why Are Tables in Excel Useful?

We can quickly sort and classify data by selecting it from the table's header. The table may easily be expanded or contracted by adjusting the rows and columns. The usage of built-in subtotal functions reduces the need to rely on formulae. Because the formula gets full of the neighboring cell, you must use the equation for all cells in the row.

Easy customization is possible with the PivotTable. There is no need for complicated formulae in this case. In the table field, there are several choices to choose from. With the PivotTable, we can compute quickly since we do not have to use any complicated formulas. When working with a PivotTable, we may make quick changes to how data is shown. Even though we can create many views from a single PivotTable, we should. The precision with which PivotTables calculate has earned them widespread use. Because of the built-in functions, the precision of the calculations is quite good.

9.4 Smart Tables Which Expand as Data Is Entered

Click on the Insert tab of the Ribbon, choose the Table button from the drop-down menu. The Create Table dialogue box is shown as a result of this step. Click the icon Create Table dialogue box, ensure the table's range includes the first row of the specified range and that the first row of the specified range is a header row. To make the changes take effect, click OK.

9.5 Creating an Excel Table from A Set

You may use a table to visually arrange and analyze data by creating and formatting it.

1. Choose a cell from inside your data.
2. Click Home, then Format as Tables from the drop-down menu.
3. Decide on a design for your table.
4. Specify your cell range in the Format from the Table dialogue box that appears.
5. Indicate whether or not your table contains headers.
6. Click on the OK button.

Chapter 10: What Are Charts?

It may be challenging to read Excel files when dealing with large amounts of data. Charts enable you to visually represent the data in your spreadsheet, making it easier to see similarities and patterns across different data sets. Several kinds of charts are available in Excel, enabling you to select the one that best suits your data. To make efficient charts, you must first grasp how they are employed in various situations. In addition to knowing the many sorts of charts, you'll need to know how to interpret a chart. Charts are composed of numerous components or pieces that may be used to aid in the interpretation of data.

10.1 A Chart Is the Set of Coordinates.

When it comes to editing and showing data, Microsoft Excel is a useful weapon, and the ability to create an x-axis and y-axis graph is a critical skill for anybody who has to present data. The scatter chart is the only form of graph in Excel that displays the XY values for a data collection on a graph; the bar chart. On the other hand, scatter charts are rather simple to understand if you have the correct sort of data on your spreadsheet. You must have data compatible with one another to create an Excel plot of X vs. Y values. When creating a scatter chart, each point is defined as one X value and one paired Y value. As a result, you'll need two columns or rows of data where the two surrounding points are connected. To create an Excel plot with XY coordinates, use the same procedure.

Suppose you have a two-dimensional collection of coordinates, such as the longitude and latitude of various places. In that case, you may plot the positions of objects on a two-dimensional plane using this information. Plotting the longitudes of various places in the first column to plot onto the x-axis with their latitudes in the two columns so that it is plotted onto the y-axis, adding negative values if required, is an example of this. To achieve the best results, use a "Scatter with just Markers".

10.2 A Compression Algorithm Is A Chart

For example, spreadsheet systems like Microsoft Excel are often thought of as tools for bookkeeping and budgeting exclusively. Even though they provide capabilities for visualizing, illustrating, and describing diverse phenomena and conducting experiments, their usage is restricted by this narrow perspective. With the help of Excel, you can express yourself in various ways when interacting with the program. As a result, Excel provides a lightweight, adaptable, and inspirational framework for developing visualizations and meeting various other objectives in Computer Science. A teacher may prepare visualizations for use in the classroom, or they can be assigned to students as homework. We present eight visualizations from the field of computer science.

10.3 How To Make An Excel Chart

To insert a chart, follow these steps:

1. Choose the cells you wish to chart and the column names and row labels from the drop-down menu that appears. These fields will contain the information that will be used to create the chart.

2. Select the required Chart command again from the Insert tab by clicking on it. The column will be used as an example in this section.

3. From the drop-down menu, choose the chart type you want to use.

4. The selected chart will be put into the spreadsheet as a separate page.

When you're not certain which chart style should be used, the Suggested Charts command will recommend different charts depending on the data you've entered into the charting tool.

Chapter 11: Excel and Our Everyday Lives

Excel makes it possible for people and organizations to complete complex computations in a short amount of time. Microsoft Excel is a very well respected spreadsheet application in the world. This section aims to explain the different applications of Excel throughout our daily lives. Some applications of MS Excel are as follows.

11.1 Solving Arithmetic Problems

The ability to do bulk arithmetic computations in Microsoft Excel is maybe the most crucial feature of the program. Because it has a large number of equations, it can do operations on hundreds of numbers at once and can simply redo operations if a value is altered or an additional value is entered. Spreadsheets for a company's annual sales and other information can be created quickly with this tool.

11.2 Formatting Alternatives

Businesses may use several formatting choices, such as italics, underlining, and colors, to distinguish the most significant information from the rest. Many things may be accomplished with this remarkable tool, like complete row highlighting and matching lists and values, to mention a few examples. You may use them to draw attention to certain entries in your accounting records.

Richard Wilson

11.3 Accessibility to the Internet

Excel is a component of the Office 365 Office Apps, which means that company owners and their staff may effortlessly access their files via a cloud network without worrying about file transfer restrictions. You can use the same application and access the same file from any web-enabled PC, mobile device, or tablet. This makes it simple to make changes if you cannot reach your PC and need to transmit the spreadsheet instantly!

11.4   Charts for Statistical Analysis

When working in a huge organization where the boss requires a thorough visual depiction of the various areas of the company, you will be required to create charts. Microsoft Excel makes it simple to do so! With a simple click, you can convert your data into a Pie Graph or tightly grouped Columns once it has been properly filtered and submitted. The colors and limits of charts and pie graphs may also be customized, a great feature!

11.5 All Information in One

Bring all the information together in one spot. Excel spreadsheets may include more than 1,048,576 rows & 16,384 columns apiece, with dozens of them, or even more if your computer is competent, in a single file, allowing you to generate spreadsheets larger than 20 A1 sheets; of paper! Through the insert tab, you can import data from other spreadsheets and also add photographs and other objects, making it simple to consolidate all of the information you've gathered in

85

numerous files into one location.

11.6 Human Resource Management (HRM)

Although alternative systems, such as Oracle or QuickBooks, may be used for planning, Excel enables you to handle everything in one document! You can immediately see a summary of an employee's spending, their hourly compensation, and any mistakes that have been made. Human Resource Professionals utilize this to gather the whole employee diary in one place and anticipate new credits and choose whether or not to spend more in the company, making it critical for future control.

Chapter 12: Formatting

Inbuilt functions for data formatting may also be used to automate the process of data formatting in Excel. In this situation, users do not need to be concerned with one-line process or other aspects. The whole section is intended to be of assistance to the user. Take advantage of a filtration editing strategy to enhance your work.

It may be used to limit a list to discover certain data sets.

Cells that fulfill certain requirements are indicated in yellow.

a) Select the cells you wish to bring the viewer's attention to.

b) From the Format option, choose Conditional Formatting from the drop-down list.

c) Select one of the given options from the list:

    i. Then, choose the comparison phrase and enter a value in the appropriate box to use values in the chosen cells as formatting criteria. i. Click Cell Value is, select the comparison term, and then type a number in the relevant box to use values from selected cells as formatting criteria. It is possible to input a constant value or a formula. You must begin a formula with the equal symbol (=) if you want it to be recognized.

    ii. Go to Formula and click it. For example, suppose a formula on the left is chosen. In that case, it should be entered in the box on the right to utilize the formula as a formatting requirement to analyze data or a condition other than the values in selected cells. It is required that the formula return either TRUE or FALSE as logical values.

d) Select the format option

e) Decide on the font type, color, underlining, borders, shading, and patterns that you'd want to employ in your document. Excel only applies the specified formats if the cell value fits the condition or if the calculation yields TRUE in the case of the formula.

To add another condition, click Add and repeat steps 3 through 5 until all conditions have been added.

12.1 Characters, Colors, Size

In Excel Spreadsheets, a user may modify the appearance of text in any cell by changing the font type, size, and color and by making it bold, italicized, or underlining. They may also modify the color of the backdrop of a cell and the border surrounding a cell. Excel's font and cell format bars are shown in the accompanying image, which explains each choice.

12.2 Alignment, Merge, Wrap

In this section, we will talk mainly about Text alignment, Merging the cells, and wrapping text in a group of merged cells.

Text Alignment

- Content in a cell should be aligned.

- Choose the cells containing the text you wish to be aligned with.

- On the Home tab, select one of the alignment choices from the drop-down menu:

- Top Align, Middle Align, and Bottom Align options for vertically aligning text.

- To align text horizontally, choose Align Text right, Align Text Center, or Align Text Left from the Align Text drop-down menu.

Merging the cells

If you wish to combine cells in Excel, pick the cells you would like to combine, press the Merge list arrow, and choose a merge option from the drop-down menu.

- Choose the cell or cells that you wish to align.

- Choose the appropriate vertical alignment button from the drop-down menu to vertical-align cells.

- Choose the horizontal alignment button from the drop-down menu to align cells horizontally.

How can I Wrap text in a group of merged cells?

Select the merging cells in which you want the text to be wrapped. Right-click the cell and then pick "Format Cells" first from the popup menu that appears.

When the Format Cells box displays, choose the Alignment tab from the drop-down menu. Make sure the "Wrap text" option is selected.

The width of the row, which includes the combined cells, will need to be manually increased or decreased when you come to the spreadsheet after this. This may be accomplished by hovering your mouse cursor at the bottom of the row until a double arrow pointing pointer emerges. Then, while holding down the left mouse button, move the cursor downward. When the row has reached the required height, click and release the left mouse button.

By viewing the content of the merged cells, it will be possible to see that text has wrapped around the cell borders.

12.3 All Cell Data Types And Common Issue

The worksheet in Excel 2022 is comprised of a grid of rows and columns that are grouped to make cells. Labels, values, and formulae are the three types of information that may be entered into cells. Text in Excel is aligned to the left-hand side of the structure. Whenever a text block is too broad to fit inside a cell, Excel stretches the contents beyond the cell width if the cell after it is blank. If the following cell does not have a blank space, Excel displays just enough text to fill the width of the display. Increasing the width of the column shows extra text.

1. Labels (textual) describe bits of information that incorporate alphabetic letters. Examples of labels (text) include names, months, and other distinguishing facts.

2. Raw integers or dates are most often used as values (numbers).

3. Formulas are directions for Excel to follow to carry out the computation.

4. In Excel, if the input is a whole number, such as 36 or 5783, the data is aligned to the right-hand side of the cell.

5. If the data contains a decimal value, Excel will align the information to the right side of the structure, such as the decimal point, excluding a trailing zero. For example, if you type in 246.75, the number 246.75 will be shown; if you type in 246.70, the number 246.7 will be displayed.

6. Using the date format 12/16, December 16, or December 16, 2010, Excel automatically returns types in the cell in your normal date format (16-Dec, if you haven't altered it), yet the Formula bar shows 12/16/2010.

To input data into a column in Excel 2022, you must first select the cell, type the data, and hit the Enter key. Excel advances the cell pointer one cell to the right. It's also possible to input data by selecting the Enter key (the checkpoint) in the Formula bar. You will only see the checkmark if you add (or modify) data.

12.4 Conditional Formatting And Table Format

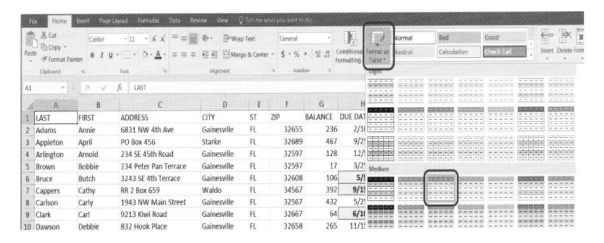

It is possible to make trends and patterns in your data more visible by using conditional formatting. You can set rules to govern the format of cells depending on their values, as seen in the following quarterly temperature readings with cell colors according to the values of the cells. You may apply conditional formatting to any variety of cells (either a selected range or a named range), an Excel table, and even a PivotTable report in Excel for Windows.

- Quick Analysis is a function that allows you to apply specified conditional formatting on the currently selected data by pressing the Quick Analysis button. When you pick data, the Quick Analysis icon shows on the screen immediately.

- The data you wish to format conditionally should be selected. The Quick Analysis icon appears in the bottom part of the selection.

- Click on the Quick Analysis button or use CTRL to do a quick analysis.

- The Formatting tab will appear in the pop-up window that displays. Move your cursor over the various formatting choices to get a Live Preview of your content, and then select the formatting type you wish to use.

Table Formatting

Excel may be formatted by the user using the tools accessible in the Font group of the Ribbon. Font styles, fill colors, and borders are all available. When we build up the format ourselves, we have to be cautious not to move cells around too much. It is quite simple to mistake the border format or the fill color. You may fall in love with Tables if you're looking for a structured structure with constant colors.

How to make a table structure:

1. Go back to Cell A1 and repeat the process (Ctrl Home).
2. Select Format as Table 3 from the Home tab, located beside the Conditional Formatting option. Choose a color scheme that alternates between the colors in each row.
3. Excel should pick up the complete dataset. That option will be left ticked since we already have titles and headers. To view the outcome, click on the OK button.
4. The conditional formatting is still in effect for the DUE DATE section.
5. We have a tab on the ribbon that will allow us to change the table's design.

6. Experiment with various table style choices and table layouts to observe how they affect the overall format of the table. The Total Row is one of the most useful features.

7. After you have enabled the entire row option, scroll to the bottom of the data. The number 77 reflects the number of records we have. Change the Total for the BALANCE row to Sum by clicking within the Total for the Balance column.

12.5 Add And Remove Columns/Cells

On the overview worksheet, arrange each category into a table with a header that corresponds to the grouping.

- Select Format as Table again from the home menu and place a click on column A3 (Items) (Ctrl-T).

- Select a table style that corresponds to the year.

- To accept the range, click OK.

- Repeat steps 3 and 4 for cells F3 (Items) & K3 (Items).

- Select cell C7 and enter the letter D.

- Hit Enter to advance to cell C8, where you should type E and press Enter.

- Right-click on Cell F6 and choose to Add a row below from the context menu.

- Repeat the process once more.

- Fill in the blanks with B and D in the relevant places.

- Find the little blue box with a backward L in the bottom right corner of N6 and press it.

- Move the box back to two rows by dragging it.

- Fill in the blanks with D and E in the relevant places.

- In Row 7, observe that you cannot Insert or Delete text by right-clicking on the header of Row 7.

- These must be completed from the interior of each table.

- Choose Cells C7 and C8 from the drop-down menu.

- Right-click - Remove the rows from the table

- Repeat the process for each table.

- F7 and F8 key

- K7 and K8

- Alternatively, undo all of the newly inserted rows.

Conclusion

The revised Excel models provide all you need to begin and go to the next level of professionalism, as well as a slew of useful features. MS Excel helps you save time by identifying patterns and organizing the data. Formulas may be entered into spreadsheets quickly and simply using models either from scratch, and current features can be used to do computations. It consists of both fundamental and sophisticated applications that may be utilized in almost any corporate setting. The Excel database allows you to quickly and simply create, access, update, and share data with others. You may create worksheets, datasets, data logs, budgets, and other documents by reading and modifying excel files that have been attached to emails, among other things. When you have a better grasp of different definitions, you will be able to identify the new features and capabilities that Excel has to offer its users, which will make your job easier. The fact is that Excel's capabilities can be tailored to meet the needs of practically any person or organization.

It would be beneficial to extend your knowledge and abilities. The learning curve for growing your talents may be overwhelming at first, but with practice and time, you will discover that things become part of a routine to you and that you no longer need to think about them. After all, repetition is the key to improving skills. Mastering these fundamental Excel abilities is what you need to achieve in order to make your job simpler, and maybe impress people around you at your place of employment. Keep in mind, however, that no matter how acquainted you are with this useful tool, there is always something new to learn about its operation. Regardless of what you do, maintain honing your Excel abilities. Not only will they assist you in keeping track of your personal earnings, but they may also open the door to a better work opportunity in the future. To summarize, knowledge is frequently referred to as being powerful, and there is no better way to drive yourself than by polishing your abilities and increasing the value of your organization via expertise and technological advancement.

Made in United States
Troutdale, OR
09/09/2023